FATI

by Glynn MacNiven-Johnston

Apostle to the Lepers

*All CTS booklets
are published thanks to the
generous support of its Members*

CATHOLIC TRUTH SOCIETY
PUBLISHERS TO THE HOLY SEE

Fr Damien shortly before his death, Courtesy of Hawaii State Archives

Fr Damien's missionary route.

Contents

Introduction 5
Early life 7
   Growing up in Belgium 7
   From farm to seminary 9
   Longing to be a missionary 11
   Bound for Hawaii 13
   Setting up parishes 14
   Catechising and building 17
Work in the leper colonies 20
   A call to the leper colony 20
   An invitation 22
   Early work and reputation 25
   Isolation 28
   Medical and pastoral efforts 31
   'I make myself a leper with the lepers' 33
   Fr Andrew and Fr Albert 34
   Recognition from Hawaii's Royal Family 35
   Reputation and controversy 36
Towards the end 39
   First signs of leprosy 39
   Brother Joseph and other companions 42
   Edward Clifford 44
   Dying poor among the poorest 47
   Controversy and honours after his death 49
   Fr Damien, disciple of Christ 50
   Leprosy (Hansen's disease) 53
Glossary 56

INTRODUCTION

It would be easy to think of Fr Damien de Veuster, the 'Apostle to the Lepers' of Hawaii, as a social reformer - and he did reform. He devoted his life to a situation which was so horrific that perhaps only comparison with the concentration camps can accurately describe it, and he made a difference through years of battling with the authorities, who were not monsters but whose priorities were different. Truth to tell, he might not have had to battle with them so much if he had had a different personality but then if he had been different he would not have gone there and he would not have stayed. Damien was by no means a perfect person. By all accounts he was very difficult to be with because he expected of others what he did himself, although he always asked forgiveness of those he had hurt. Now he is on the way to canonisation, to being declared a saint. This means that in some way his life reflected Jesus Christ. But in what way?

Fr Damien's life shows that there is no degradation which can separate us from the love of Christ, and there is no suffering where He is not present. It shows us that anyone's life can be transformed by God; that we should not be afraid to embrace the life that He has given us, nor feel destroyed when we find ourselves unequal to the events and situations we have to face. Damien made huge changes in the leper colony, huge improvements, but he could not take away the leprosy. What he did was to help make Christ present in that situation and many of the leprosy sufferers discovered meaning in their suffering. More than any medical or social work, Damien's gift lay in his becoming a leper for the lepers, rejected for the rejected - like Christ Himself. They, in turn, discovered their own vocation - to share in the redemptive suffering of Christ, and this is finally what changed everything for them. This is very hard for us to understand perhaps for our generation more than for others, because our world wants to eliminate suffering, to make everything clean, perfect and beautiful. Damien's life was a challenge to his contemporaries, and it challenges us too.

EARLY LIFE

Growing up in Belgium

Fr Damien was born on 3 January 1840 in the village of Tremeloo near Louvain in Belgium, the seventh of the eight children of Frans and Anne de Veuster. He was named Joseph and called Jef for short. The de Veusters were a farming family, by no means rich but not poverty stricken either. Frans de Veuster grew and marketed grain. The family's Catholicism and the practice of their faith were woven into the fabric of their daily lives. Anne de Veuster especially was a deeply religious woman, and it was from this background that two of the daughters entered a convent and two of the sons became priests. There were also to be religious vocations among the grandchildren. Jef was only 5 years old when his eldest sister Eugenie took her vows as an Ursuline nun and 11 years old when she died in a typhus epidemic. At that point Pauline, the next sister, chose to enter the same convent 'to take Eugenie's place'. This made a strong impression on Jef which was to be very important later on.

At the end of the nineteenth century, when Fr Damien first became famous, saints were usually portrayed as totally perfect, and a story began to be told of Jef, to illustrate his 'saintly piety' even as a child. The story is that one day he disappeared and his distraught family, after looking everywhere, finally found him deep in silent prayer in the local church. The parallels with the child Jesus being found in the temple are unmissable but in case you do miss the intended comparison with Jesus this story is sometimes coupled with the information that he enjoyed looking after the family's flock of sheep. The truth of the incident is a little more human. Jef was a popular boy and was usually to be found with a whole gang of other village boys, one of whose favourite games was to jump onto the back of a fast-moving cart. The boys would wait for a cart to pass and one of them would jump onto the back and hold on to the tailgate. To make sure that it was moving fast enough, the other boys would throw stones at the horse to make it bolt. By the time the carter had got the horse under control, the boy had had a dangerous and exciting ride. The boy would then run off while the carter was still calming the horse. On this particular day it was Jef who jumped on to the cart, but the horse failed to bolt. The carter stopped it at once and seeing and recognising Jef, shouted after his fleeing figure dire threats of informing his parents. Jef had heard that sanctuary could be claimed by fleeing criminals in any church, and that is why he went there. His parents did find him inside the altar rail deep in prayer - a prayer he had begun as soon as the door opened. Frans and Anne were pious people and could not hit him in church nor even shout at him, so they had to resort to hissing at him

FATHER DAMIEN

to come out. Jef was nothing if not stubborn and he finally rung out of his parents the promise that he would not be punished. Only then did he accompany them home. On the whole, however, Jef was a quiet boy. In fact, the neighbours called him 'Silent Jef', but this was not a sign of timidity: he was the local speed skating champion. Nor was he withdrawn. His letters to his parents when he was away at school show that he was open, demonstrative and affectionate.

From farm to seminary

Jef left school at thirteen to work on the farm. He also helped the village blacksmith who doubled as local gravedigger. Jef was of average height but very broad and strong. When he was only thirteen, he could lift 100 kilo sacks of grain as if they weighed nothing. He was quite happy on the farm, but Frans wanted to do the best for all his children and for the family as a whole. It was decided that Jef should go to business school to learn better ways of marketing the family grain. The school was in the French-speaking (Walloon) part of Belgium. The fact that Jef spoke only Flemish was not considered an insurmountable problem so, when he was sixteen, Jef was sent to school in Braine-le-Compt in Hainault. The first few months must have been very difficult. He spoke no French and had never been away from his family before, but he did not complain. He wrote to his family: 'It is with great pleasure that I take pen in hand to write to you a short letter for the first time. By now I am quite accustomed to this place. I talk to the Walloons a little. I know my work, my lessons, my companions, and my bed. Everything in the house is clean and comfortable. Our table is like the one at the annual fair and the beer is very good. Any Walloon that laughs at me I hit with a ruler.'

Whilst in Braine-le-Compt, Jef went to a retreat organised by the Redemptorist Fathers and there he heard a call to the religious life. He wrote to his parents that he wanted to become a Trappist monk. This was a complete surprise to his parents, who thought of his brother as the priest of the family. (Jef's elder brother, Auguste, a brilliant student, had entered the Congregation of the Sacred Hearts of Jesus and Mary, taking the name Pamphile.) They thought it must just be a phase and told him to wait and reconsider. Jef then asked his brother, Pamphile, who was very supportive, and with the help of the parish priest managed to convince their father to allow Jef to try out his vocation. In 1858, at the age of eighteen, Jef entered the same Congregation as his brother and took the name Damien after the fourth-century saint and doctor. (Incidentally, it was in a church dedicated to St Damien that St Francis of Assisi had heard Christ's call to rebuild his Church.) The Congregation accepted Jef only after much deliberation and then only as a brother, not as a candidate for the priesthood. He had already been refused outright by the American College at Louvain who did not see in this rough and burly farmer the kind of candidate for the missionary priesthood they wanted. The report of his interview says he was rude and obviously uneducated in Latin or anything else. Damien did not protest at the position he was given, but he asked his brother, Pamphile to read Latin with him during recreation, and Pamphile, the kind of man who loved learning for its own sake, agreed. When he saw how seriously Damien was studying and how determined he was to learn, Pamphile approached the superiors of the seminary and asked that his brother be admitted as a candidate for the priesthood. Strangely they agreed, although they made his novitiate two months longer than anyone else's just to be on the safe side.

Longing to be a missionary

Damien was happy as a seminarian. He took as his motto: 'Silence, recollection and prayer' - and to remember it better he carved it into the top of his desk with a knife. Damien was enthusiastic but calm, and his superiors were won over by his modesty. He felt that the other seminarians were much more intelligent and spiritual than he was. Studying did not come easily to Damien. He was only an average student but he had great determination and perseverance. He prayed every day for the grace to become a missionary, in front of a picture of St Francis Xavier, who was one of his heroes. Damien's novitiate photograph shows him standing in a pose very like the portraits of that saint.

God wastes nothing, and the French that Damien had learned in Braine-le-Compt was put to good use when he was sent for a time to the motherhouse in Paris. There he made his profession on 7 October 1860. Part of the ceremony involved the candidates prostrating himself, covered in a black pall, before the altar, symbolising his free acceptance of his death to the things of the world. This ceremony was later to take on an even deeper meaning for Damien. Damien liked being in Paris, though he was not so impressed by the promenading ladies and gentlemen and fashionable carriages, which he complained got in the way of his walks.

In 1863 Pamphile was chosen as one of a group of missionary priests to go to Hawaii, then called the Sandwich Islands, but a few weeks before the group was to go, he caught typhus and, although he survived, it was obvious that he would not be well enough to sail with the others. Remembering how his sister Pauline had felt, called to take his sister Eugenie's place when Eugenie had died, Damien offered himself in Pamphile's place. He did not ask anyone's advice nor did he ask the rector of the seminary. Instead he wrote directly to the Father General of the Congregation. In his letter he added that this would also mean the ticket money would not be wasted. To everyone's amazement, since Damien was not even yet ordained, the Father General agreed. However, the rector of the seminary made sure he berated Damien for his forwardness and recklessness before he told him he was allowed to go.

Bound for Hawaii

The suddenness of this decision meant that Damien only had time for a brief visit to take leave of his family. He also stopped at the shrine of Our Lady of Montaigu to ask her protection. So, at the age of only twenty three, Damien left with the group of nine priests and ten missionary sisters to sail from Bremerhaven in Germany. From there he wrote to his parents: 'Do not trouble yourselves in the least about us. We are in the hands of God... who has taken us under his protection. All I ask is that you pray for us to have a good voyage and that we may have the courage to fulfil our mission. This is our life. Good-bye, my dearest parents. We will never have the happiness of seeing one another again in this life but we will always be united by our love for one another and in our prayers.' The voyage to Hawaii was round Cape Horn as the Panama Canal had not yet been completed. It took five months, and most of the group spent all one hundred and forty six days being seasick. Damien spent it trying to convert the Protestant crew with no success at all.

On 19 March 1864, Damien arrived in Hawaii, and was ordained a few months later, on 21 May 1864, in the Cathedral of Our Lady, Queen of Peace in Honolulu on the island of Oahu. He said his first Mass in the same cathedral. Damien and a companion, Fr Clement Evrard, were then to begin their lives as missionary priests on the island of Hawaii after which the whole island group is now called. So, accompanied by Bishop Maigret, they boarded a steamer to make the journey. They stopped off at the island of Maui and then had to stay there longer than expected as the steamer caught fire. Damien did not want to waste any time so he received permission to go out to the villages to say Mass, hear confessions, and to preach. The latter he did in broken Hawaiian, which everyone was too polite to tell him was incomprehensible. When he returned from the villages he found that Bishop Maigret and Fr Clement had gone on ahead so he sailed on alone finally catching up with the bishop on 24 July in the parish that was to be his own.

Setting up parishes

As a parish priest, Damien was energetic and resourceful, supporting himself by farming, raising livestock and growing tobacco. He kept bees for honey and wax to make the church candles. He found his parishioners enthusiastically Catholic except when they were being enthusiastically Presbyterian or Mormon or when they were ill - then they called in the local sorcerer. He wrote to his brother: 'If only Providence had sent a Curé of Ars (St John Vianney) here, all the stray sheep would have returned to the fold... Pray that Fr Damien will give himself completely to God and devote himself to His service to his last breath. To have begun is nothing, the hard thing is to persevere. This is the work of God's grace. That grace will never fail me, I am sure of that, provided

I do not resist it. Pray for me... Continue to pray for the conversion of unbelievers. It is probably to your fervent prayers that I owe the conversion of 40 to 50 pagans and heretics that I baptised this year.' Damien was a man of his era and he did not yet have an ecumenical spirit. He delighted in a kind of rivalry with the Protestant missionaries, whom he lumped together as 'heretics'. Once he heard that a local Protestant minister had climbed a 700 metre cliff in two hours so he ran up the same cliff in forty-five minutes. Fr Clement, meanwhile, who was not as robust as Damien, was finding his much larger parish, with an area of about 1600 square kilometres, too difficult. They decided it would be more sensible to change over, and their superiors agreed.

Much of Fr Damien's life in his second parish reads like a *Boys' Own* adventure story. One of the villages he wanted to visit was so isolated that he decided the best way to get there would be by outrigger canoe across the sea. He set off with a few of his Hawaiian parishioners but after quite a short time the canoe capsized in the high waves and he and the others found themselves in the water. He wrote home prosaically that they managed quite easily to swim back to shore as they held on to the capsized canoe and each of them took turns to beat the sharks off with the paddles. Nothing was lost, but his breviary was damaged beyond repair by the salt water, which he regretted. He decided he needed to recover from this and gave himself a week before setting off again.

This time he went on foot. He made the journey, which proved to be four days long, with a huge rucksack strapped on his back in which he carried a 'portable' altar which he had designed and made himself. He had to wade and swim through the sea at various points and then he came to a small mountain. He decided to climb it holding on precariously to plants and stones and in the process cutting his hands and feet on the sharp volcanic rock. When he reached the top he found himself looking down into a ravine with no sign of any village. He climbed down into the ravine and, since he had come that far, up the other side. By this time his boots had been ripped to bits and his hands and feet were torn and bleeding. On top of that the rains had begun and his way was now further hampered by mud, sometimes waist deep. There was still no sign of a village, but Damien had been assured it was there so he started down the second ravine and then up the third mountain. It was now too late to go back, he decided. At the top of the third mountain he still saw no sign of any village, even in the distance, but he started down into the next valley. There he collapsed with exhaustion and exposure and lay unconscious in the pouring rain. He would have died there had he not been found by the very villagers he was searching for. They revived him and he was so overjoyed at seeing them that he was soon able to walk to their village, which in fact was quite close by, if not visible from where he had collapsed. As soon as he had rested a little he began to help with the work in the village, to the astonishment of those who had found him and thought him on the brink of death. He began to catechise and many of the villagers accepted his preaching. Before he left he helped the villagers build a church, 'not a sort of hut as most of our chapels are but... built entirely of wood.' He put a two metre-high cross on the top.

Catechising and building

His vitality, zeal for the proclamation of the gospel, and love of life were inspiring and exhausting. In the seven years he was in this parish he built four small churches with his own hands. 'I play the carpenter when necessary and have a good deal of work in painting and decorating my chapels. In general I have much bother and little consolation', he wrote, but he was in his element. This is not to say he did not have bad times. He found it hard to be so long without the sacrament of reconciliation, to find another priest he had to make a journey of 100 kilometres, and he got very depressed by the level of drunkenness and the resulting casual sex amongst his parishioners. But he came to admire and respect the Hawaiians very much, writing to his brother: 'You could not wish for a better people, so gentle, pleasant and soft hearted... They do not seek to amass wealth... They are exceedingly hospitable and are ready to deprive themselves even of necessities in order to supply your every need if you should ask a night's shelter of them.' The Hawaiians (who, having no *"d"* in their alphabet, pronounced his name Kamiano) also liked him and he began to make many converts. He was, however, very careful not to baptise lightly.

Neither was everyone so welcoming of Christianity. On the islands there was also a form of voodoo which kept many of Damien's parishioners in fear and at the mercy of its practitioners. Damien decided to discover who the members of the secret society were and to put a stop to it. Being Damien, he dealt with it head on. He had discovered an altar of this cult and destroyed it. Then he made a large cross by tying together two branches and drove it into the ground where an idol had stood. The next day he found a small bundle tied to his door. This was an evil spell, a curse. The whole village was watching what he would do so he untied it from his door, carried it contemptuously over to a large pig and tied it to its tail. By the evening the pig was dead, although it had been helped on its way by someone who had slit its throat. Damien butchered the carcass and cooked it, but no-one would share it with him. That night a woman warned him that his life was in danger. Damien did not wait for them to come to him. Returning to where he had seen the altar, he found the witchdoctor and many of the villagers. They had sacrificed a dog and were pouring out its blood. There on the altar was a doll dressed in a cassock and with Damien's rosary round its neck. Damien rushed forward, grabbed the doll, pulled off its head and throwing it to the ground, stamped on it. Everyone waited for him to die but he did not. 'You are not children.", he said, "Why are you afraid of dog's blood and a doll?'

After this there was little opposition to him. He swept through the district with indefatigable energy, building, reforming, setting up schools and even getting help from the government to train Hawaiian women as teachers. Damien also survived a tsunami (tidal wave), a hurricane and a volcanic eruption. He wrote to his family that there was nothing like an erupting volcano to give you a good idea of hell.

During these years on Hawaii, Damien had hoped that Pamphile would one day join him. The brothers often wrote to each other about that, and Pamphile had asked many times to be allowed to do so but had never been given permission. Then he was offered and accepted a university post. Damien was hurt and furious and wrote a bitter letter to Pamphile accusing him of not having the courage to be a real priest. The brothers became estranged over this and it lasted almost three years - probably so long because there was nothing like a postal service in Damien's parish and he had to depend on others passing by and going on to Honolulu in order to send a letter. But finally Damien was able to send a letter begging forgiveness and the correspondence between them was resumed.

Work in the Leper Colonies

A Call to the leper colony

A few years after he had arrived in Hawaii, Damien wrote home: 'Leprosy is beginning to be very prevalent here. There are many men covered with it. It does not cause death at once but it is rarely cured. The disease is very dangerous because it is highly contagious.' It seems that leprosy first arrived in Hawaii with the Chinese indentured labourers, brought there to work on the plantations. It spread rapidly amongst the Hawaiians, who had no immunity and who were extremely hospitable, which to them meant being together all the time, eating from the same dish, wearing one another's clothes, smoking each other's pipes and so on.

Leprosy was, and still is, a terrifying disease. The body begins to rot away while the person is still living. The symptoms are varied but often nodules appear on the skin which then become ulcers. The nose may collapse, the eyes become infected and pulpy. The face can become a single hole as the nose and mouth are eaten away. Or the sufferer can become disfigured as their skin thickens and forms ridges. The disease can also destroy the nerves so that the person no longer has any feeling in that part of their body. Sores form and the extremities of the body begin to break off. These days the disease can be halted and it is known that only some forms of the disease are infectious, and these are not considered to be highly contagious, but in Damien's day ideas about leprosy had scarcely changed since Biblical times.

By the mid-nineteenth century, as a result of increasing pressure from the white settlers on the islands, drastic measures were being taken to control the disease. King Kamehameha V signed the 'Act to Prevent the Spread of Leprosy' on 3 January 1865. Sufferers were to be sent to Molokai, one of the smaller islands, lying between Oahu and Maui. Its geography made it perfect for quarantine. It is about sixty-five kilometres long but only twelve wide and slopes up from north to south, the land ending suddenly in a cliff that runs the whole breadth of the island. At the bottom of the cliff there is an area cut off from the rest of the island and surrounded on three sides by water. It was here that the lepers were to be segregated.

Enforcing this law was not an easy task for the authorities. The Hawaiians were averse to giving up their loved-ones and often hid them until armed police were sent to forcibly drag them off. There was a great deal of resistance, and the police often ended up shooting as many people as they managed to round up. These were herded onto a ship which sailed to the south end of Molokai where they were dumped in the shallow water off the island and left to wade ashore as best they could. Even children had to fend for themselves. At first it was decided that the lepers should be sent to Molokai not as patients but as settlers. This made economic sense, though no other kind of sense, and the first group, of nine men and three women, who reached there on 6 January 1866 were sent with farming tools and seeds. They were expected to be self-sufficient. It soon became clear that it was ridiculous to expect such ill people to do this, so the scheme was abandoned. Patients were then given one set of clothes a year and minimal supplies which were simply thrown into the water with the incoming new sufferers and left to be fought over. There was a hospital building but no doctor or medical equipment, and they had to build their own shelters.

In the midst all this horror was a small wooden chapel dedicated to St Philomena, a saint the Curé of Ars had a particular devotion to, where some of the Catholic leprosy sufferers would gather to pray, especially the rosary. This church had been built by a Sacred Hearts brother, Brother Bertrand and a Hawaiian helper in 1872. (There was also a small Congregational church which had been built a year earlier.) In the past, three different priests had made short stays on the island, but the lepers felt they needed a full-time priest and this was the request they put to the bishop.

An invitation

In 1873, Damien received an invitation from Bishop Maigret to the dedication of a new church at Wailuku on the island of Maui, and to greet a new group of priests who had just arrived on the islands. He did not take much with him as he did not expect to be away long. He was with the bishop when the letter from the lepers in Molokai arrived. Four priests volunteered to go, including Damien. He was under no illusions about what this meant. He later wrote: 'Monsignor Maigret declared that he would not impose this sacrifice on any of us. Remembering that on the day of my profession I had already put myself under the funeral pall, I offered myself to his lordship to meet, if he thought it well, this second death'. He asked that one of the newly arrived priests be sent to his parish and that he be allowed to go to the leper village which was called Kalawao. It was decided that the four priests would serve there in rotation for periods of four months at a time. Damien was to be the first to go. He left with the bishop for Honolulu, and on their arrival there, they found that fifty lepers were being sent to Molokai that evening. It seemed the perfect opportunity. So the bishop and Damien sailed with them. Damien had no time to get any of his belongings, and went to Kalawao with only the clothes he was wearing, his breviary and an extra shirt. He arrived on Molokai just before dawn on 10 May 1873. The bishop landed with Damien and spoke to the lepers who had gathered round saying to them: 'I have brought someone to be a father to you; someone who loves you so much that... he does not hesitate to become one of you; to live and die for you.'

He found no words to say to Damien but he laid his hands on Damien's head to bless him, then he had to get back on the boat. Damien was alone.

He went first to the church and set at once to work to clean it After some time a man came and offered him some fruit and later another came with some flowers to decorate the church. He then saw a small group of people carrying a dead body and he took it upon himself to conduct a funeral - the first of very many. There was nowhere for him to live so he spent that night and the subsequent ones under a tree. He later wrote:

'By special providence of Our Lord, who during his life on earth showed a particular sympathy for the lepers, my way was traced to Kalawao (Molokai)... I was then 33 years old and in robust good health... A great many lepers had lately arrived from the different islands; there were 816. Some were acquaintances of mine but to the majority I was a stranger... They were all living at Kalawao - about eighty of them in the hospital. All the others were living further towards the valley. They had cut down the puhala groves to build their houses though a great many of them had nothing but the branches of castor oil trees to construct their shelters. These frail frames were covered with sugar cane leaves or grass. I myself sheltered under the pandanus tree which is still in the church yard. Under these primitive roofs these unfortunate outcasts from society were living pell-mell without distinction of age or sex, old and new cases together all virtual strangers to one another. They passed their time playing cards, dancing the hula and drinking home-made alcohol... Under the influence of this liquor they would neglect everything else except dancing and prostitution. Since they had no spiritual advisor they were hastening down the road to complete ruin. Many of those who were prostrated by the illness were left lying there to take care of themselves and some of them died for lack of help while those who could have helped were going around searching for enjoyment of the most immoral kind.'

When Damien arrived in Kalawao the average life expectancy for a leper, once he or she arrived in the settlement, was four years. About fourteen new sufferers arrived every week and there were four to five deaths in the same period.

Early work and reputation

In the outside world, Damien became controversial as soon as he landed on Molokai. A Honolulu newspaper wrote that he was permanent chaplain to the lepers (this was news to the civil authorities) and called him a Christian hero. As soon as Fr Damien heard this he wrote to ask his provincial if he could in fact be made permanent chaplain and since he was also always practical, he asked in the same letter for altar wine and hosts, spiritual books, clothes, flour and a bell. Another article appeared in the Honolulu Advertiser, this time about his living under a pandanus tree and donations started coming in from all the islands (mainly from Protestants) which allowed him to build himself a hut about five metres long and three metres wide. All this acclaim galled the Protestant missionaries, and they began to write their own articles about Protestant ministers who had visited Molokai. It also annoyed the Board of Health whose authorisation for Damien to stay on the island had not been requested.

Damien, meanwhile had begun his ministry. He visited the bedridden, hearing confessions, administering Extreme Unction (Sacrament of the Sick) and washing and bandaging their sores. He did not find this easy at first. The sight and above all the smell of lepers' decaying flesh turned his stomach, and he often had to rush out of the shelters and vomit. The first time he administered Extreme Unction on the island horrified him. When he came to anoint the man's feet he found them already full of maggots. He began to smoke a pipe continuously to overcome the smell. He wore boots because he suffered a psychosomatic itch on his legs when he was with the patients and he suffered terrible headaches from the stress. Even in celebrating the Mass he found great difficulty. He fought to overcome his nausea in the crowded church by thinking of Christ at the tomb of Lazarus. Gradually though, he became more used to it. Later, visitors were always amazed at his tenderness and skill as he looked after the lepers.

It was not until he had been on Molokai for six months that he found time to write to his brother: 'I have been here six months and I have not caught the infection. I consider this due to the special protection of God and of the Blessed Virgin. Leprosy is incurable... Discoloured patches appear on the skin, especially on the cheeks and the affected parts lose their feeling. After a time this discolouration covers the entire body and ulcers begin to open. The flesh is eaten away and gives out a fetid odour; even the breath of the leper is so foul that the air is poisoned by it. I have had great difficulty in getting accustomed to such an atmosphere... Now my sense of smell does not cause me so much inconvenience. I enter the huts of the lepers without difficulty. Sometimes I feel no repugnance... Picture to yourself a collection of huts with eight hundred lepers. No doctor; in fact, as there is no cure, there seems no place for a doctor's skill.'

The terrible conditions were made much worse by the lack of fresh water. There was no water in Kalawao and it had to be carried from some distance away. Those who had lost the use of their hands or feet could die of thirst. Water was so scarce that there was none to be wasted on cleaning. Damien began by carrying water. Then he began his first battle with the Board of Health. He had found a natural reservoir of water and he wanted pipes to bring water into the settlement. He bombarded the authorities with letters and pipes were sent, but without workers to lay them, and the lepers, for the most part sunk in the inertia of despair as well as being crippled, were in no fit state to help. Finally Damien cajoled the seamen on whose ship the pipes had come to help him lay them. The captain of the ship was a Hawaiian with the unlikely name of John Bull. Between them, Bull and Damien made plans and the seamen and some of the lepers helped them lay the pipes. With water piped into the village and standpipes set up, life improved immeasurably.

Damien's care did not end with the living. One thing that had distressed him very much was the way the dead were just tossed over a small cliff and left to be eaten by the wild pigs and dogs. Even those who were lucky enough to have someone to bury them ended up being dug up by scavenging animals, as their graves were so shallow. Damien built coffins and dug graves. He made a cemetery which he called the garden of the dead and he prayed for them. Being practical, he also set up a little savings scheme so that the lepers could put some money away towards a coffin.

Isolation

Molokai was not an otherwise uninhabited island. There were people living on the main part of the island but, other than by boat, the only way off the peninsula was straight up the cliff. A later visitor described the ascent: '(The cliff) was almost perpendicular; it crumbled as we clung to it like cats and when I looked below to find footing I discovered that the rock upon which I was stretched in agony of suspense was apparently overhanging the sea... I nearly fell from sheer fright.. I tried to forget that I was suspended in mid-air by my eyelids with nothing but sole leather between me and a thousand feet of space with certain death at the lower end of it. We were rained upon and shined upon, covered in dust and debris and when we reached the top, I was dizzy and parched with thirst...We made it in two hours forty minutes with my heart knocking wildly at my ribs all the way up.' This did not deter Damien. He made the ascent as often as he was able, to minister to the Catholics on the rest of the island.

Some time after Damien's arrival on Molokai there was a storm, and all the shelters that had been built at Kalawao were destroyed. Damien saw that this would be a good chance to ask the Board of Health to do something constructive, something they could not refuse. He would ask for timber to build proper shelters. He took the opportunity to travel to Honolulu to visit his bishop, make his confession, and to visit the Board. The Board of Health already did not like Damien, and Damien did not deal well with bureaucracy or delays. The meeting did not go well. Damien lost his temper and the president of the Board, who was by now convinced that Damien was a rude, officious busybody, reminded him that he was only on Molokai to minister to the spiritual needs of the Catholics in the leper colony, not anything else. He should not be interfering in the running of the colony. Furthermore, since people were forbidden from leaving

Kalawao, he should not be going to Molokai Topside (the main part of the island) and he should definitely not be visiting Honolulu. If he was going to remain in Kalawao, he must obey the quarantine. Damien declined to do so. The Board enforced it as far as they were able. But he got the wood for new houses. Back on Molokai he began building small huts. Once the lepers had seen what was possible, they began to build too and soon small houses appeared everywhere. In time they also had gardens, growing flowers and vegetables, and soon they were selling potatoes to the Hawaiian government. The people who feared any contact with the lepers themselves somehow were not afraid to eat the potatoes they had grown. This helped the lepers earn some money and gave them more independence and self-respect.

For some time, Damien was not able to leave the island, nor was anyone allowed to visit him. Again, his greatest suffering was not being able to receive the sacrament of reconciliation. Furthermore, he had joined a Congregation because he did not really want to be alone. Things came to a head when Damien's provincial, who was deeply aware of this need, boarded a ship to Molokai intending to spend a few days with Damien keeping him company and hearing his confession. But when he arrived at the island, the captain of the ship refused to let him land. Damien, seeing this, got into a small boat and rowed out to the ship. The captain refused to let him board. Damien was distraught, but since they had come this far he decided the only thing for it was to shout his confession from the boat to his provincial on the ship. And this is what he did. The ship was already pulling away as his confessor shouted back his absolution. Reports of this reached the ears of the French consul, who was quite scandalised and made an official protest to the Hawaiian authorities. Because of this, the ban was lifted. Later Damien also received companions although as things turned out this was not always an undiluted pleasure.

Medical and pastoral efforts

Meanwhile Damien continued to work for the lepers. There was no doctor at that time, so Damien got some medical books and began to do what he could. He often found that he had to amputate limbs which had become infected. There was no anaesthetic but it was not needed, as the patients had lost all feeling in the affected part. There were also no gloves to protect Damien from the pus-filled limbs he was removing. A naval surgeon who visited said Damien had become quite expert at amputation having done it so many times. He continued his conflict with the Board of Health, complaining to them that the lack of bandages meant that many wounds could not be dressed and this was responsible for the spread of other diseases. The Board finally sent a few basic medical supplies. They also sent enough stock to set up two shops - one in Kalawao and the other in Kalaupapa. Kalaupapa was the second leper colony which had grown up at the other end of the peninsula. Of course Damien built a church there. He also enlarged St Philomena's Church - in fact he had to do so twice - because it was too small for the congregation. He decorated it so that it would be cheerful and appeal to the congregation. This was something of a shock to Europeans. One of the Franciscan sisters who later joined Damien on Molokai, said it looked like a Chinese shop. He also made the Mass as ceremonial as possible. He wanted everyone to feel involved and uplifted. He formed various associations, choirs which became quite famous, and an orchestra. The orchestra played very well despite the fact that 'the musicians had for the most part only two or three fingers and their lips were very much swollen'. The Feast of Corpus Christi was celebrated with great ceremony. Damien described to his brother that there was a procession headed by a cross 'followed by a magnificent banner, the brass instruments and drums come next. Two Hawaiian flags wave over two rival associations. Long files of women are next, then the men marching in rows then a choir of forty voices under the direction of my good blind Petero... the thurifers and children who scatter flowers...' The ceremony was followed by a meal in which everyone shared. 'You see that Our Lord lets us now and then pick a beautiful rose among sharp thorns.' He also encouraged horse-riding and racing as these were things that most of them could do even in the late stages of their illness, and arranged barbecues and fishing competitions.

'I make myself a leper with the lepers'

Damien was not on Molokai simply to make this life easier for the lepers. He was also concerned with their eternal life. Damien identified with the lepers from the beginning. Very early in his time there he wrote: 'As for me I make myself a leper with the lepers to gain all to Jesus Christ. That is why in preaching I say "We lepers" not "My brothers" as in Europe.' He had many conversions but he did not administer baptism lightly, and so he trained teams of catechists from among the lepers to give instruction. He also formed two associations, one of men and one of women, whose purpose was to bring comfort and help to the needy. He himself spent long hours in the confessional. Leprosy often attacks the vocal cords, reducing the voice to a hoarse whisper and Damien had to lean very close to the penitent to hear what was being said, very close to the leper's breath with its terrible smell. Worse than that, some were afflicted with fits of coughing which sprayed Damien with blood. This was so common, he used to take a towel and a bowl of water with him into the confessional. In both churches perpetual adoration was introduced. The lepers were very faithful to this. If they were too ill to go to the church, they would make the vigil in their homes. They had found that in their suffering there was a dignity. In their suffering they met Christ and were enabled to offer that suffering for the salvation of others.

Fr Andrew and Fr Albert

For six years Damien worked alone on Molokai then a Dutch priest, Fr Andrew Burgermann, who had been working in Tahiti, was sent by the Congregation. Damien was at first delighted by Fr Andrew's arrival. He was happy to have a companion and he hoped that Fr Andrew could care for the spiritual needs of the other parishioners on Molokai, those outside the leper colony. But Fr Andrew had other ideas. He had some medical training and felt he was much better suited to looking after the leprosy patients than Damien. Their superiors seemed to agree, so it was Damien who was sent up to minister to the other parishioners. Soon relations between the two men were very strained. Damien was difficult and demanding, and Fr. Andrew was not only ambitious but a little unbalanced. He decided at one point to leave the order and abandoned all religious duties, working only as a doctor. When Damien argued with him about this, Fr Andrew threatened him with a gun. After two years Fr Andrew left Molokai, but he did not leave the order. This inability to live in harmony with a member of his own congregation counted against Damien with his superiors. Damien did not want to be without companions, but when they arrived he was unable to live with them.

The next to arrive was Fr Albert Montitor. Fr Albert had been in the South Pacific for twenty-four years and was something of a celebrity. He was sent to Molokai because their superiors had begun to have serious reservations about Damien. He was considered rude, bad-mannered and rash, and now rumour circulated about his morality. Of course Damien was happy to stay on Molokai, his enemies said. After all it was well known that leprosy was a result of syphilis. Lepers were obviously immoral and Damien was surely having unrestrained sexual relations with the women of the leper colony. Fr Albert seemed convinced of the truth of these accusations before he had ever met Damien. The first thing he did when he arrived at the settlement was to get rid of all the women who worked anywhere near the priest's house. Then he told Damien of the rumours about him and preached and nagged at him so much and for so long that Damien asked that Fr Albert be sent somewhere else. This was refused, as was his request to visit Honolulu (to get some respite). Finally it was Fr Albert's health which saved Damien. Severe eczema necessitated his seeking treatment in Honolulu. He decided not to return to Molokai. Like his predecessor, Fr Albert had only been able to tolerate Damien for two years, although, for the rest of his life, he would not hear a bad word about Damien and became one of his fiercest defenders.

Recognition from Hawaii's Royal Family

In 1881, King Kalahua, who was the last Hawaiian monarch before Hawaii was annexed by the United

States, went on a world tour leaving his sister, Princess Liliuokalani, as Regent. The Princess was a very capable woman who took advantage of her brother's absence to institute many reforms. One of the things she decided to do was to visit the leper colony. Damien and his parishioners wanted to do their best for their distinguished guest and they painted, cleaned and covered everything in flowers. Everyone who was able to do so came to the landing stage to welcome the Princess. There was music, a guard of honour, everything they could think of. When the time came for her to make a speech, she could not. She could only cry. She was overcome by the tragedy and the horror of the place. But she did not want to disappoint them. She went on a tour of everything and stayed the whole day instead of the hour which had been scheduled. As she was leaving she asked Damien how he was able to stay, but he only answered that these people were his parishioners. Some time later the bishop came to visit, bringing with him the jewelled insignia of the Royal Order of Kalakaua and a personal letter from Princess Liliuokalani.

Reputation and controversy

In the outside world, as the years passed, Damien was becoming ever more well-known. This was in part due to his brother Pamphile who would pass Damien's letters on to the Congregation's newsletter for publication. Damien was not happy about this and wrote to his brother: 'I was a little annoyed to find my last letter printed in Annals.

Once and for all let me say that I do not want that to be done. I want to be unknown to the world and now I find I am being talked about on all sides even in America.' Pamphile ignored him and there was nothing Damien could do. The news in turn was picked up by other papers worldwide. In England, Reverend Hugh Chapman, who was an Anglican vicar of St Luke's Church in Camberwell, London, was inspired by Damien's apostolate and wrote offering to raise funds for the colony. Damien was very happy to allow this and Chapman set to work with great enthusiasm, speaking to his parishioners and writing articles for the national newspapers. Soon letters began to appear in the press, some were in support but many were against. The controversy makes little sense to the modern ear, but was typical of its time and quite fierce. One letter said that Damien, far from helping, was making moral lepers of the patients and leading them straight to hell with his terrible Catholic propaganda. Others said the lepers would be better off dead than in the clutches of Rome. Still others believed that Damien was interfering with God's will - the lepers were moral degenerates who had been struck down with the disease because of their debauched lives and needed to suffer to atone. Chapman was undaunted. He enlisted the aid of Cardinal Manning, the then Archbishop of Westminster, and in three years Chapman and his parishioners had raised and sent over two thousand pounds to Fr Damien - a very great deal of money in those days. The money, the honours and the publicity that Damien received made his superiors even more uneasy about him. The publicity was embarrassing for the Hawaiian government also, as it made it seem that they were neglecting the lepers and that it was left to foreigners to fulfil what was really their responsibility, when in fact Hawaii was spending a larger percentage of its revenue on caring for lepers than any other country. This did not help relations between the authorities and the Sacred Hearts Missionaries as a whole. Damien's superiors began to wonder if he really was seeking publicity and honour for himself. This critical attitude of his superiors upset Damien a great deal.

Towards the End

First signs of leprosy

In 1885, when he was forty-five years old and had been a missionary for half his life, Damien heard about the work of Mother Marianne, a German-born American Franciscan, who with six other sisters, had recently come to the Islands to help care for the lepers. They had founded the Kapiolani Home for the care of lepers in the grounds of Honolulu hospital and the Hawaiian government had asked Mother Marianne if she would be prepared to open another home on Molokai. Fr Damien went to see her in early July 1886, and from all accounts 'Silent Jef' exhausted everyone with talking. He was particularly concerned that she and her sisters take care of the children. Children who contracted leprosy were sent to Molokai alone and afraid. There were also children who were born on the island and whose parents subsequently died. Damien, very aware how vulnerable they were, had founded two small orphanages - one for boys and one for girls. He was very much concerned about what would happen to them when he died because now he knew he had leprosy himself. The year before, he had written to the Father General in Rome, 'I have been decorated with the Royal Cross of Kalakaua and now the heavier and less honourable cross of leprosy. Our Lord has willed that I be stigmatised with it... I will keep on working.'

From early on in his apostolate Damien had lived in close contact with the lepers in the Hawaiian manner. A visitor wrote: 'The pipe was filled and passed to him although just removed from a leper's mouth. He ate out of the family calabash.' His detractors with the prejudices of the time said he had 'gone native', but he answered that all he was doing was winning souls for Christ using the methods of St Paul - being all things to all men. Damien first suffered pain in his left foot which soon made walking difficult, then the pain spread up his leg. A little later he had an accident where he put his foot into scalding water and realised he could feel nothing. By October 1885 he was sure and he wrote to Fr Leonor Fouesnel, his superior: 'I am a leper. Blessed be God. I only ask of you that you send someone into my tomb to be my confessor.'

Some time later Pamphile contracted tuberculosis and wrote to tell Damien of it. Damien wrote back: 'As for me I can't hide from you for long that I am threatened by an even more terrible disease. As you know leprosy is contagious. I'm still as healthy as ever at the moment but I've had no feeling in my left foot for the last three years... I have a poison in my body which threatens to spread through it. But let's not shout about it. Let's pray for one another.'

He made light of his symptoms and his mother was not told of his illness. He had always tried to spare her the worry of his being in Kalawao, and earlier he had written to reassure her 'I live alone in a little hut; the lepers never enter it. In the morning after Mass a woman who is not a leper comes to prepare my meal. My dinner consists of rice, meat, coffee and a few biscuits. For supper I take what was left at dinner with a cup of tea. My poultry yard supplies me with eggs. After dark I say my breviary by the light of my lamp, study a bit or write a letter, so don't worry that I don't write often. I only really have time to remember you in my prayers.' This was true when he wrote it. But in 1884, Dr Mouritz, the doctor the Board of Health had finally, that year, appointed to Kalawao, described Damien's house as 'Kalawao Family House and Lepers' Rest, free beds, free board for the needy...'. In fact he was stunned by Damien's indifference to segregating himself from the sick. In early 1886 news of Damien's leprosy got into the papers in a sensationalized account which said his flesh was falling off in chunks. His mother, who was now eighty-three years old and a widow for thirteen years, read this and was horrified. She became silent and withdrawn and began to waste away. She died shortly afterwards on 6 April.

Added to the loss of his mother, Damien now suffered what seemed to him the loss of his Congregation. He was still alone and now he had leprosy. He wrote to his superiors that he wanted to come to Honolulu - to meet

Mother Marianne - but also to find comfort with his brothers of the Congregation. Fr Fouesnel wrote back asking him not to come to the missionary headquarters but to stay at the hospital with the sisters. 'But if you go there,' he added, 'please do not say Mass. Neither Fr Clement nor I will celebrate Mass using the same chalice and the same vestments you have used. The sisters will refuse Holy Communion from your hands.' This apparent harshness is understandable given how infectious leprosy was thought to be and how careless Damien seemed to be, but Damien spoke of this 'rejection' as the greatest suffering he had to endure in his life. He shared with Christ not only physical suffering but this harrowing loneliness and abandonment.

Brother Joseph and other companions

But God had not forgotten him. On 19 July 1886 Damien received a companion. Ira Dutton was an American in his mid-forties, a convert from Episcopalianism. He had read about Fr Damien in a magazine and felt inspired to go there. He, however, did not want to make any rash decisions. He visited the author of the article to make sure. Only then did he set out for Hawaii, where he went to see first the bishop and then the head of the Board of Health. After all this he asked to go to Molokai as a volunteer - in fact, he was hired by the Board of Health who were very impressed by him. Dutton was a man who had known suffering of his own. After fighting in the American Civil

War and a disastrous marriage to a woman who spent all his money and then went off with another man, Dutton had become an alcoholic. He was an alcoholic for many years. But in 1883 he stopped drinking and was converted to Catholicism. He changed his name to Joseph. He spent some time in a Trappist monastery and they would have accepted him as a monk, but he felt God was calling him to something else. This something else was Molokai, and he worked there for forty-five years, until he died in 1931.

Damien was very happy to have Dutton with him. He soon began calling him 'Brother Joseph'. Damien built him a small house and gave him a lot of work. Brother Joseph was astonished at the amount of work, the number of projects - they often worked from dawn until midnight. But Brother Joseph never complained. He was well known for never losing his temper or showing any sign of impatience no matter how much provocation there was. There was real communion between himself and Damien. Brother Joseph wrote: 'Fr Damien had in his heart when tranquil a most tender feeling as I often have been made to know. You will bear me out in stating the fact that no one found it pleasant at all times to be with him for a very long period. If my intimate association with him was longer continued than others, it was partly because I admitted my own faults in that regard, and partly because I ever saw him place in me the most entire confidence and have in his heart a deep love no matter what his exterior might be. And also I used to be quite open with him in speaking of all these things; he likewise to me, and this seemed to give us confidence in each other.'

Later another 'brother' arrived. This was 'Brother James'. James Sinnet was an Irishman who had been hired by the Board of Health. He arrived the year before Damien's death, and developed a total devotion to him. It was he who nursed him at the end and after Damien's death he could not bear to stay on Molokai. Just before James Sinnet's arrival, Damien finally received his confessor. Fr Lambert Conrardy came to work with Damien. He too was a Belgian, but was a secular priest not a member of the Sacred Hearts Congregation. He had wanted to come to Molokai for some time but had not received permission from Damien's superiors who would have preferred a priest from their own congregation. Fr Lambert stayed on Molokai for six years after Damien's death, then he left to study medicine. He qualified as a doctor and went to work in a leper hospital in Canton. He died there in 1914, not of leprosy but of pneumonia.

Edward Clifford

In 1887, Edward Clifford, an artist, read a magazine article about Fr Damien. He was going to spend some time in India and decided to visit Damien on his way back to England. He arrived there at Christmas 1888, bringing with him a large number of gifts and some considerable donations of money from various sources. The gifts were in a huge packing case which proved impossible to land, so Clifford unpacked the case on the ship and passed the contents out one by one. There was gurjun oil, which Clifford had seen used to relieve some of the suffering of leprosy in India. There were engraved Stations of the Cross for the church, a magic lantern complete with slides of scenes from the Gospels, and there was a barrel organ which played fifty different tunes and was the star of the Christmas celebrations. There was also a painting, by Burne Jones, of St Francis receiving the stigmata, and sent by the artist himself. Damien was overawed at the value of this gift but he was thrilled by the subject (St Francis also had great compassion for lepers) and placed it in his own room. He could see it from his bed when he was dying and it comforted him.

Clifford and Damien took to each other at once, and they spent a happy time together discussing all sorts of things including religion. Clifford, an Anglican, was surprised at how much they agreed on, because, as he himself admitted, he was rather anti-Catholic and as a child had been terrified at the sight of Catholic nuns, who he was sure would kidnap him to use in horrible rituals. He said of Damien: 'I was glad to find in conversation with him that it was no part of his belief that Protestants must be eternally lost.' Damien had changed from the early days of competition among missionaries. Clifford made some sketches and watercolours of Damien whom he described like this: 'He is now forty-nine years old - a thick set, strongly built man with curly black hair and a short beard turning grey. His countenance must have been handsome with a full well-curved mouth and a short straight nose; but he is now a good deal disfigured by leprosy though not so badly as to make it anything but a pleasure to look at his bright sensible face. His forehead is swollen and ridged, the eyebrows are gone the nose is somewhat sunk and the ears are greatly enlarged.' When Clifford showed him one of the drawings and asked if he would like it sent to his brother, Damien said: 'What an ugly face. I didn't think or know that the disease had made so much progress.' He said he thought it would be too great a shock for Pamphile to see him like that. Clifford's niece, in a letter to *The Times* in 1932, says she thinks this is why Clifford made an idealised portrait of how he thought Fr Damien must have looked as a young man for the front of the book he wrote in 1889. This idealised portrait was very popular and was reproduced again and again but as Clifford's niece said it was 'rather an expression of... love and veneration... than an actual portrait of Fr. Damien.' When Clifford left, Damien gave him a card with pressed flowers from the Holy land and when Clifford asked Damien to write something in his Bible, he wrote: 'I was sick and ye visited me. J. Damien de Veuster.' He did not want to be pitied. He said: 'I am the happiest of missionaries. I would not be cured if the price of my cure was to give up my work and leave the island.'

Dying poor among the poorest

The disease now made rapid progress. Marks and sores appeared on his face, one of his arms swelled beyond recognition and was so heavy it had to be carried in a sling. His nose collapsed which made wearing his glasses difficult, he had acute diarrhoea and he felt desperately tired. He had difficulty walking. But worst of all, his larynx was affected. He could not breathe if he lay down so sleep became almost impossible. He would wake up coughing. Melancholia is a common symptom of leprosy, and Damien became profoundly depressed. He believed he had failed in the mission God had entrusted to him and that he was not worthy of heaven. Night after night he would walk through the cemetery, praying the rosary, praying for the souls of the dead and asking them to pray for him. He started to go blind but he struggled to continue saying the Divine Office. He had bouts of fever. Then he received news that Mother Marianne and the sisters had arrived along with their priest, Fr Wendelin Moellers. He got out of his bed to meet them. This he said was his 'Nunc Dimittis' (Luke 2,36). He could now depart in peace. His lepers would be cared for.

He wrote a last letter to his brother: 'I am quite happy and contented, and though seriously ill all I desire is the accomplishment of the holy will of God. I have a priest from Liege with me, Fr Conrardy, and Fr Wendelin is in another village. Besides these I have two brothers who help me in the care of a hundred orphans who are in my charge. The hospital contains over a thousand lepers. We also have sisters here; three Franciscan nurses... I am still able but not without some difficulty to stand at the altar every day where I do not forget to pray for you. In return, please pray and have prayers said for me who am being gently drawn towards the grave. May God strengthen me and give me the grace of perseverance and a happy death.'

In March 1889 he became bedridden. He made his confession to Fr Wendelin and renewed his religious vows. He also made a will giving to the bishop all the donations that had been given to the leper colony. He was happy to own nothing, 'not even a firm grasp on life'. Fr Wendelin said: 'He seemed so happy.' Damien knew the signs of death well. The open wounds were healing and the crusts turning black. 'I would so like to have seen the bishop again,' he said 'but never mind. God, is calling me to spend Easter in heaven.' On 2 April, Fr Conrardy gave him Extreme Unction. 'God is good to have kept me alive until I had two priests with me', Damien said. But even at the end Damien was not sentimental. Fr Wendelin wrote: 'I asked him to leave me his mantle as Elijah did so that I would have his big heart. "What would you do with it?" he asked, "It's full of leprosy!" I then asked him for his blessing. He blessed me with tears in his eyes and blessed the sisters too, for whose coming he had prayed so much. What I most admired in him was his admirable patience. He who was so ardent, so alive, so strong... to be nailed in this way to his sickbed... Like the poorest of lepers, he was lying on the ground on a poor straw mattress and we had a lot of trouble getting him to accept a bed.' In fact he only did so because they told him it would be easier to nurse him on a bed than on the floor. Then they found he owned no sheets. On 15 April he died. It was Holy Week. Those who were with him said he simply gave a childlike smile and 'died without any effort'.

He was dressed in his cassock and white vestments. Requiem mass was said by Fr Wendelin and eight patients carried his coffin to where he was buried under the pandanus tree he had slept under, those first nights on Molokai.

Controversy and honours after his death

But even in death he was not free from the attacks of his enemies. A few years after his death Dr Charles Hyde wrote to a colleague, Rev Mr H B Gage. In his letter Dr Hyde said that Fr Damien was given honours he did not deserve. He had contracted leprosy because of sexual relations with the island women and he had died because of his carelessness and his corruption. It was divine retribution. Gage had the letter published and it was soon read round the world. Robert Louis Stevenson, the author, who had visited Molokai in 1889 and had been very impressed with it though he had been too late to meet Fr Damien, was scandalised by this and wrote a scathing attack on Hyde accusing him of envy and hypocrisy and claiming he had lost the last shreds of honour and decency. Stevenson saw to it that this was published throughout

America and Europe. The newspapers were only too glad to have a battle like this to attract readers. But Hyde did not have the same ability to express himself as Robert Louis Stevenson, and he was silenced until four years later when Stevenson died. Then Hyde claimed that, before his death, Stevenson had accepted Hyde's interpretation of events - something Mrs Stevenson denied.

In 1935, the Belgian government made a formal request for the remains of Fr Damien to be returned to Belgium. The United States government (Hawaii was by now an American territory) agreed and Fr Damien's body was disinterred on 26 January 1936 and taken to Honolulu where the coffin lay in state in the cathedral for several days before being put on a ship to Belgium. The ship arrived at Antwerp on 3 May and it was met by King Leopold III, dignitaries of church and state and thousands of ordinary people. All the church bells were rung. The coffin was taken to Antwerp Cathedral on a hearse drawn by six white horses for a solemn commemoration before being taken to Louvain, where his body was placed in a black marble crypt in St Joseph's Church. His empty grave remained open in Molokai.

Fr Damien, disciple of Christ

The cause of Fr Damien was opened by Pope Pius XII in 1956. There was so much documentation that it took years, and it was not until 7 July 1977 that Pope Paul VI declared Damien was of 'Heroic Virtue' and he was given the title Venerable. In 1991, it was accepted that a miracle had been obtained through Damien's intercession. This was the cure of Sister Simplicia Hue, a French religious whose fatal illness had disappeared after she had begged Fr Damien's help. The date for Fr Damien's beatification was set for 5 May 1994, his crypt had been opened and his remains placed in several zinc boxes, when Pope John Paul II suffered an accident where he broke his leg and the ceremony was postponed until 4 June 1995. It took place outside the Koelkelberg Basilica in Brussels in torrential rain. Along with King Albert II, 500 priests and 40 bishops, was Mother Teresa of Calcutta, a long-time admirer of Fr Damien. Also there, were a number of former patients from Molokai - patients continued to be sent there right up until 1949. Hawaiians, Europeans, Americans, members of the Sacred Hearts Congregation, lay people, all stood for hours in pouring rain to honour him. One group of English Sacred Hearts Sisters remained saturated all day. In fact, when they returned to England their shoes took four days to dry out but not one of them became ill - a blessing they attribute to Fr Damien. The Mass of the beatification reflected both the European and Hawaiian cultures and the Pope spoke in French, Flemish, English and Hawaiian. and designated 10 May as Blessed Damien de Veuster's feastday. This was the date Fr Damien first landed on Molokai. The Pope was presented with an twenty-five-metre-long scroll with the prayers of thousands of Hawaiians asking for Fr

Damien's intercession. One of the zinc boxes, which contained a relic of Fr Damien, was returned to the Hawaiians, Cardinal Danneels saying: 'Brothers and sisters of Hawaii, we return to you the relic of the right hand of Fr Damien who blessed and healed many people in your country. May it continue to be a source of blessing and comfort and a symbol of our love and solidarity with you.'

The relic was later re-interred on Molokai by Fr Bukoski, the superior of the Sacred Hearts Congregation, during a ceremony of great celebration.

In his beatification address Pope John Paul II declared: 'In order to give definitive confirmation to the truth of his witness he offered his life in their midst. What could he have offered the lepers who were condemned to a slow death if not his own faith and the truth that Christ is Lord and God is love? He became a leper among the lepers; he became a leper for the lepers. He suffered and died like them believing that he would rise again in Christ for Christ is Lord!... Blessed Damien, you let yourself be led by the Spirit as a son obedient to the Father's will. In your life and in your missionary work you show Christ's tenderness and mercy for every man, revealing the beauty of his inner self which no illness, no deformity, no weakness can totally disfigure. By your actions and your preaching you remind us that Jesus took on himself the poverty and suffering of mankind and has revealed its mysterious value. Intercede with Christ physician of soul and body for our sick brothers and sisters so that in their anguish and pain they may never feel abandoned but that in union with the risen Lord and with his Church, they may discover that the Holy Spirit comes to visit them and they may receive the comfort promised to the afflicted ...'

Leprosy (Hansen's disease)

Contrary to popular belief, leprosy has not been eliminated. There are currently at least six million known cases ('Hansenians' or 'Leprosy sufferers') in the world; over two million people suffering from the active disease and four million others who are disabled and disfigured because of it. The stigma of leprosy is such, however, that there are many more cases which remain unreported. Some estimates put the true number of sufferers as high as twelve million. Ninety five percent of known sufferers are in Bangladesh, Brazil, Burma, India and Nigeria, but it is not specifically a tropical disease. Leprosy reached epidemic proportions in Europe in the Middle Ages. The last native British person to suffer from the disease in Britain was a Shetland Islander who was diagnosed in 1798, but there was an outbreak in Scandinavia in the nineteenth century and there are still known cases in the USA, Spain and Eastern Europe. It is possible that leprosy has virtually vanished in the richer countries due only to improved housing and nutrition and reduced exposure to other diseases and parasites. The fact is that much about leprosy remains a mystery.

Medically, leprosy is now known as Hansen's disease after Gerhardt Hansen, a Norwegian, who isolated the leprosy bacillus, a germ similar to the one which causes tuberculosis, in 1873. When Damien was on Molokai the best available treatments for leprosy sufferers were soothing baths and gurjun oil applied to the sores. This approach having not changed very much since Biblical times, remained the only one for many years. An African-American chemist called Alice Ball discovered that derivatives of chaulmoogra oil were effective, but the first major breakthrough in treatment did not happen until 1946, with the discovery of a sulphone-based drug, dapsone. This drug was found to halt the progress of leprosy. If treated early enough, patients did not suffer the disfigurement and loss of limbs which are symptomatic of the later stages of the disease. Since 1982, leprosy has been treated with multi-drug therapy, which is generally dapsone in combination with other drugs. Those drugs vary depending on how the disease manifests itself. With this treatment the progress of leprosy can be halted within six months in those patients with the less serious forms of the disease. Treatment takes two years for those who have the more serious, infectious form. The average cost of treatment is currently just over twenty pounds per person. This has made a dramatic impact and it was hoped that, with education, the stigma of leprosy would be removed, more people would come to the clinics and be treated, and the disease would, like smallpox, be eradicated.

However, a great many of the sufferers are in isolated and inaccessible regions, and in some areas progress has been further hampered by wars and natural disasters and AIDS. Also in the 1990s, it became clear that the bacterium was becoming resistant to dapsone and even to the other, newer drugs used in multi-drug therapy, making the World Health Organisation's stated goal to eradicate leprosy by the year 2000 an impossibility.

There is no vaccine against leprosy and its mode of transmission is still uncertain. It generally takes prolonged and close contact with an infected person for the disease to be transmitted, but whether or not a person exposed to the disease contracts leprosy depends largely on his or her immune response. The disease is more common in men than women, but again it is not known why. Normally, leprosy has an incubation period of between two and five years, but it can be much longer. It has been known for someone to have leprosy for thirty years before exhibiting any symptoms, and it is difficult to know whether the disease has been cured or is simply in remission. For the foreseeable future it is estimated that there will be approximately 600,000 new cases each year, of whom 100,00 will be children.

Glossary

Beatification: The act by which the church recognises and permits the honouring of a person who has died with a reputation for holiness, or who has suffered a true martyrdom. The Pope does not however, definitively declare that the person is already in glory.

Canonisation: After an exhaustive process of inquiry into a candidates life and works and the verification of miracles obtained through the candidate's intercession (not necessary in the case of a martyr) the Pope decrees that the candidate is already in heaven and that the candidates name be inscribed in the book of saints and be venerated in the universal church.

Extreme Unction: This sacrament, now known as Anointing of the Sick involves the anointing by a priest, of the head and hands of the seriously sick, but not necessarily moribund person with oil blessed by the Bishop.